BOY SCOUTS OF AMERICA
MERIT BADGE SERIES

FISH AND WILDLIFE MANAGEMENT

 BOY SCOUTS OF AMERICA.

Requirements

1. Describe the meaning and purposes of fish and wildlife conservation and management.

2. List and discuss at least three major problems that continue to threaten your state's fish and wildlife resources.

3. Describe some practical ways in which everyone can help with the fish and wildlife conservation effort.

4. List and describe five major fish and wildlife management practices used by managers in your state.

5. Do ONE of the following:

   a. Construct, erect, and check regularly at least two artificial nest boxes (wood duck, bluebird, squirrel, etc.) and keep written records for one nesting season.

   b. Construct, erect, and check regularly bird feeders and keep written records of the kinds of birds visiting the feeders in the winter.

   c. Design and implement a backyard wildlife habitat improvement project and report the results.

   d. Design and construct a wildlife blind near a game trail, water hole, salt lick, bird feeder, or birdbath and take good photographs or make sketches from the blind of any combination of 10 wild birds, mammals, reptiles, or amphibians.

6. Do ONE of the following:

   a. Observe and record 25 species of wildlife. Your list may include mammals, birds, reptiles, amphibians, and fish. Write down when and where each animal was seen.

35898
ISBN 978-0-8395-3307-8
©2004 Boy Scouts of America
2010 Printing

BANG/Brainerd, MN
3-2010/059109

b. List the wildlife species in your state that are classified as endangered, threatened, exotic, game species, fur-bearers, or migratory game birds.

c. Start a scrapbook of North American wildlife. Insert markers to divide the book into separate parts for mammals, birds, reptiles, amphibians, and fish. Collect articles on such subjects as life histories, habitat, behavior, and feeding habits on all of the five categories and place them in your notebook accordingly. Articles and pictures may be taken from newspapers or science, nature, and outdoor magazines, or from other sources including the Internet (with your parent's permission). Enter at least five articles on mammals, five on birds, five on reptiles, five on amphibians, and five on fish. Put each animal on a separate sheet in alphabetical order. Include pictures whenever possible.

7. Do ONE of the following:

a. Determine the age of five species of fish from scale samples or identify various age classes of one species in a lake and report the results.

b. Conduct a creel census on a small lake to estimate catch per unit effort.

c. Examine the stomach contents of three fish and record the findings. It is not necessary to catch any fish for this option. You may visit a cleaning station set up for fishermen or find another, similar alternative.

d. Make a freshwater aquarium. Include at least four species of native plants and four species of animal life, such as whirligig beetles, freshwater shrimp, tadpoles, water snails, and golden shiners. After 60 days of observation, discuss with your counselor the life cycles, food chains, and management needs you have recognized. After completing requirement 7d to your counselor's satisfaction, with your counselor's assistance, check local laws to determine what you should do with the specimens you have collected.

8. Using resources found at the library and in periodicals, books, and the Internet (with your parent's permission), learn about three different kinds of work done by fish and wildlife managers. Find out the education and training requirements for each position.

Pine marten

Gray wolf

Atlantic salt marsh snake

Contents

Why Manage Fish and Wildlife?

Wildlife management is the science and art of managing the wildlife—both animals and fish—with which we share our planet. Maintaining the proper balance and the dynamics that go with it requires humankind's attention. This includes managing and maintaining wildlife habitats of all kinds.

We use this stewardship tool to help minimize or eradicate the possibility of extinction of any given species. We want our descendants to have the opportunity to experience the same animal diversity that we now enjoy. This is a role of the entire wildlife management team to which we all belong, to constantly

Millions of bison once roamed the Great Plains, but by 1884, only 300 of these massive creatures were left.

help monitor and control the factors and conditions created by humans that affect wildlife, to help wildlife adapt to what they or humans cannot change.

Throughout history, events caused by humans have greatly affected the wildlife populations of the past. We cannot change what has happened, and we cannot bring back the lost populations and extinct species of yesterday. However, with good vision and wildlife management practices today, we can help prevent similar wildlife tragedies in the future.

The Early Days

To understand the importance of fish and wildlife management, keep in mind a general concept of what fish and wildlife resources were like in the early years of this country's settlement and development. Before European colonization, most of the North American continent was a vast wilderness, pristine and pollution free, teeming with fish and wildlife wherever their needs—food, water, shelter, and living space—were available. As the settlers and civilization moved into the countryside and pushed farther and farther west, they made changes to the landscape for their benefit. These changes often were made at the expense of the indigenous (native) wildlife populations.

For example, roughly 300 years ago the uninterrupted prairies were home to vast herds of bison, estimated to number some 60 million. Species such as the bison were so heavily utilized to meet the needs of the growing population of newcomers that in little more than 100 years after settlement of the prairies, only a few hundred of these magnificent animals were alive. Another example is the passenger pigeon, at one time one of the most abundant birds in the world. This bird is now extinct because of overhunting. The last surviving passenger pigeon died in a Cincinnati zoo in 1914.

During those early days, America's lakes, rivers, and streams were free of pollutants. Our wild rivers allowed countless generations of salmon to migrate upstream, uninhibited, from the sea to their historic spawning beds. Over time, excessive sediment, chemicals and other polluting factors, and changes to the landscape have impaired water quality and wildlife habitats because of more intensive development and resource use. This includes factors such as agriculture, timber cutting, mining, transportation, and manufacturing.

A species is a classification level of organisms, such as the bison, that are capable of interbreeding and producing fertile offspring.

A marsh is an excellent habitat for a wide variety of wildlife, such as these egrets, but as Americans' need for space grew, some marshes disappeared in favor of dry land for towns and cities.

Although the loss of wetlands for fish and wildlife use continues to this day, that rate of loss has been reduced considerably over the past 10 to 20 years. Experts have estimated that between the 1780s and the 1980s, the contiguous 48 states lost approximately 221 million acres of wetlands—about a million acres per year. By the 1970s to the 1980s, that loss amounted to about 290,000 acres lost per year. Although the net loss between 1985 and 1995 had dropped to 117,000 acres per year, there still are great strides to be made toward wetlands restoration.

Anthropomorphism — Big Word, Simple Meaning

Humankind has had more influence in the loss and alteration of our country's wildlife habitat than any other factor in history. In the past, people mistakenly believed that the frontier would go on forever and that there was always more wilderness just over the next mountain. This was not the case, of course, and as the westward movement of the settlers of the 18th and 19th centuries moved onward they caused vast changes to the landscape and wildlife habitats.

Anthropomorphism means, in simple terms, regarding animals as humans.

Today, we still are causing great change in the landscape and wildlife habitats in the form of highways, dams, cities and suburbs, fences, golf courses, and airports. All of these modern-day developments affect places where wild animals and fish have lived and migrated through for many years. Pollution in our rivers and streams, intense suburban sprawl into wildlife corridors, noise pollution, and pesticide and fertilizer usage all have played a role in altering wildlife habitats.

Most people don't understand the complexities of the wildlife world. Animals and animal populations are not indestructible. From this lack of understanding has spread a misconception—anthropomorphism—that now is a plague for fish and wildlife managers. This is what makes understanding the individual life cycles, habitat requirements, and what is called the prey-predator relationship all so important.

While that might sound simple enough, remember that most fish and wild animals are potentially the "next" meal for a predator. As a result, usually far more offspring are produced than the land and water can support. This prey-predator relationship is only one very basic element in the risk of living in the wild. Disease, starvation, human actions, the weather, and natural disasters such as forest fires and flooding all play a role in the survival of animals in the wild.

A predator is an animal that survives by preying upon others.

Mountain lions

This all might make you wonder what makes the animals that concern a fish and wildlife manager different from the domestic animals we keep as pets. The most significant difference is that all of our domesticated animals live in environments controlled by humans. These animals have no need for basic food hunting skills to survive because their keepers provide their dietary needs. They do not have to test the laws of nature with regard to "survival of the fittest," reproductive competition, and seasonal migrations. In fact, our pets in general have a pretty good life compared with their wildlife counterparts.

On the other hand, animals in the wild live with some rather harsh realities. Think about what a deer in the deep snow of the Rockies would need to do to survive. Consider the salmon that is genetically "tuned" to swim hundreds of miles upstream, past hungry bears, eagles, and human obstacles just to reproduce. Envision the great annual migrations undertaken by caribou, Canada geese, and monarch butterflies just to survive.

Mother Nature (humankind's anthropomorphic term for the natural world around us) has established some stringent rules for living in her world. To survive, wild animals require food, water, shelter, and living space with their own kind; this is their habitat. Each element is specific to each species but in general they are not much different from what humans require.

We may never have the answer to every question about the best form of wildlife management for every species. It's a challenge today and will continue to be a challenge in the future. Possibly the experiences you gain from earning the Fish and Wildlife Management merit badge will encourage you to follow a career in wildlife management and help find answers to those challenges.

Enjoy the journey.

In fish and wildlife management, habitat refers to the needs—food, water, shelter, living space—a species requires for survival.

White-tailed deer

Bald eagle in flight

Basics of Fish and Wildlife Management

A number of factors affect the health and well-being of fish and wildlife, and any change in an animal's food, shelter, water, or living space can affect its ability to survive and thrive. Human actions, including practices adopted by land managers, frequently play a part in plant and animal succession, directly reflecting the health and well-being of a species. Effectively managing fish and wildlife takes an intimate understanding of animals and their environment.

At the Center—Habitat

The word might be familiar to you, but to many people, the meaning of **habitat** is foreign, or at least hazy. In fish and wildlife management it refers to the needs of any given species, or individual specimen, to survive. Those needs generally consist of proper amounts of food, water, shelter, and living space. Fish and wildlife have very specific habitat needs.

Some fish require water of a certain depth, clarity, temperature, and flow rate. Other fish require water of a totally different nature to live. Certain species of wildlife need precise temperatures, certain kinds of trees or other vegetation, and minimum or maximum amounts of sunlight.

Bald eagle chicks

Habitat needs may change drastically by season or by the age of a given animal. A young wild turkey, for example, must have a rich protein diet of insects to provide growth; later in the same year it will require berries, seeds, acorns, and similar foods. This is a case of the dietary needs of a species being well-matched to the habitat; in the spring when the birds are small, the woodland habitat of the wild turkey is teeming with insects, and in the fall the other foods the birds need in their maturity are plentiful.

Knowing the precise habitat needs of any species of fish and wildlife, and knowing how to provide these needs in certain balances, is the center of effective fish and wildlife management.

Different species might occupy the same territory at the same time because certain requirements are the same, but they might be consuming totally different food, and perhaps utilizing totally different shelter. A rabbit might find shelter in a brush pile and food in green leafy plants while directly above, a squirrel might be living in a hollow tree and eating acorns. The Animal Foods and Cover chart in this section compares the different requirements of a number of animals.

White-tailed deer

Porcupine

Animal Foods and Cover

Mammal	Foods	Cover
Badger	Ground squirrels, mice, prairie dogs, birds, eggs	Hole in ground
Beaver	Bark and twigs of aspen, cottonwood, willow, other deciduous trees; root grasses	Lodge made of saplings partially underwater, a den in a bank
Black bear	Acorns, beechnuts, grasses, roots, fruits, berries, insects, honey, mammals, birds, fish and frogs, carrion	Wooded area
Chipmunk	Seeds, nuts, acorns, berries, insects, birds' eggs, young mice	Underground nest
Cottontail rabbit	Dandelions, common plantain, lance-leaved plantain, clover, and many other types of vegetation	Brushy area
House rat, house mouse	Ragweed, lamb's-quarters, redroot, tumbleweed, foxtail, various grains and vegetation products, meat	Grasses and weeds; in house walls, litter, trash areas
Striped skunk	Insects, small mammals, eggs, snakes, crayfish, carrion	Brush along watercourses, woodlands
Opossum	Small birds, frogs, mammals, fish, eggs, insects, fruit, carrion	Trees, burrows
Otter	Fish, crayfish, mollusks, eggs, birds, small mammals	Den in stream bank with underwater entrance; hollow log
Porcupine	Bark and twigs of pines and other trees; shrubs and grown plants	Trees, brush, caves, rock crevices
Prairie dog	Grasses, weeds, roots, clover, grains	Burrows
Raccoon	Frogs, fish, shellfish, small mammals, birds, eggs, reptiles, insects, fruit, corn, nuts	Hollow trees or logs
Red fox	Mice, other small mammals, birds, fruit	Hollow logs or stumps, burrows in banks, etc.
Red squirrel	Berries, nuts, seeds, insects, birds' eggs, fledgling birds	Tree cavity, abandoned woodpecker nest; always in forest
Weasel	Small mammals and birds	Rock pile, downed log, burrow in stream bank
White-tailed deer	Twigs and leaves of shrubs, trees; mast, grasses, plants	Heavy brush, woodlands
Woodchuck	Grass, clover, crops, weeds, etc.	Wood piles, stone walls, burrows in ground

Bird	Foods	Cover
Barred owl	Birds, mice, frogs, crayfish	Tree hollow in wooded swamp or forest
Black-capped chickadee	Seeds, insects, berries, other fruits	Hole in tree, nest box
Cardinal	Seeds, grubs, beetles, grasshoppers, caterpillars, fruit	Hedgerows, trees, shrubs
Domestic pigeon	Grains, seeds, acorns	Trees, buildings, bridges
House sparrow	Grains, seeds, beetles, other insects, worms	Trees, bird boxes, buildings
Meadowlark	Caterpillars, beetles, cutworms, grasshoppers, seeds, grain	Grassy areas of fields
Mallard	Marsh plants, insects, mollusks, small fish	Freshwater marsh
Red-tailed hawk	Small mammals, reptiles, frogs, insects	Woodland
Robin	Worms, fruit	Trees, shrubs, buildings
Starling	Insects, grains, seeds	Brushy shrubs, nest boxes, tree holes

Wildlife Communities

A **food chain** shows how energy from producers is passed from one consumer to another within an ecosystem.

An **ecosystem** is a community of organisms and their environment.

Everything on Earth is interrelated, from its soil to its most magnificent creatures—humans. We take plants from the Earth to use in building our homes, making our clothes, and preparing our meals. We depend on plants to manufacture the oxygen we need to breathe. Likewise, all other animal life on Earth is dependent on plants, and those plants depend on the soil. The way humans and other large animals are linked to the soil through smaller animals and plants is called a **food chain.**

The chain starts in the soil. There plants begin to sprout, drawing on the sun's energy to combine carbon dioxide, water, and minerals from the soil to make their own food. And the plants become food for many kinds of animals, from the tiniest worm or insect to the large deer. The food chain progresses from the soil to the plant to a small animal to a larger animal. When that animal dies, its remains decay, returning nutrients to the soil to be utilized by plants.

So, plants are critical to all wildlife communities. Plant life creates a forest, a marsh, a desert, or a prairie and supports the animals that live there.

Plant and Animal Succession

Another factor that the wildlife manager must understand is *plant and animal succession.* Basically this means that when land is cleared of vegetation (by fire, lumbering, volcanic eruption, etc.), different kinds of vegetation appear in successive stages. Annual weeds appear first, then perennial weeds, then shrubs, then certain kinds of trees. Trees such as oaks, maples, and pines represent the final stage, or *climax.* Generally with each successive stage of plant growth the animal life changes also, depending on the habitat needs of various species.

As deepwater habitats (lake, river, marine) and wetlands (marsh, swamp, bog, fen, prairie) become older, they undergo a process known as **eutrophication,** a change in depth size, vegetation, and character through gradual filling. As they age, depending on the location, some habitats change to scrub-shrub

The plants that will grow in a particular wildlife community are dependent on that area's soil and climate, and in turn, so are the animals that make the wildlife community their homes.

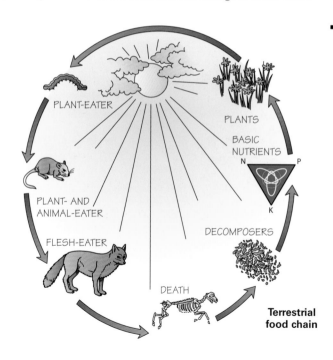

Terrestrial food chain

Eutrophication is the natural process by which a wetland becomes more mature and more productive.

wetlands, some become forested wetlands and eventually forests, and others become prairie. Succession is hastened by drainage and tillage practices that increase erosion and sedimentation.

> Wildlife managers can manipulate plant and animal succession to accommodate certain wildlife species and to discourage others. This is known as **enhancement of habitat.**

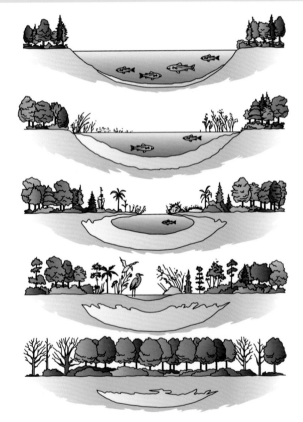

As lakes and wetlands of various types age, they tend to be filled in and replaced by prairie or forest. Humans hasten this succession by drainage and land-use practices that increase nutrient loading, erosion, and sedimentation.

A Model Community

To get an overall look at an ecosystem and its life cycles and food chains, set up a freshwater aquarium. Monitoring the aquarium over a period of time will help you get a sense of how animal species and their environment work together.

Creating an aquarium environment is not difficult, but to get the balance of life just right, everything from the water to the plants to the fish and other animals must be handled with care. For more information on setting up an aquarium, see the Pets *merit badge pamphlet.*

To start, choose a 10- to 20-gallon rectangular tank with a large surface area that will allow plenty of oxygen to dissolve into the water. Clean the aquarium with water (no detergent or soap). Place it on a level, sturdy surface away from dark corners, drafty places, or where the temperature fluctuates a lot. Place it by a southward-facing window so that the plants and animals get enough light, or use a full-spectrum ultraviolet fluorescent light on top of the tank.

Complete your aquarium by adding a cover or hood to keep the animal life in and the dirt out. Leave a small space open in the hood along the back of the tank to provide access for other aquarium equipment, such as tubes, filters, and heaters. A one- or two-bulb reflector can be mounted on the cover to provide additional light.

Line the aquarium floor with sand or gravel, sloping it upward from the back of the tank to the front. Then fill the tank with 2 to 4 inches of tap water. Allow the tank to sit for 24 hours, so that the chlorine in the water dissipates.

An easier and faster way to "age" the water is to use a commercial dechlorinator, available at pet shops. Follow the manufacturer's instructions carefully, and always use chemicals only under the close supervision of an adult.

Next, add live plants. Keep them moist while you work, and do not bury the crowns of the plants. Some plants have stems that are bunched together, and they can be planted that way. However, do not

plant individual plants in bunches. Spread the roots after you set the plants, and carefully level the gravel or sand around their bases.

The aquarium is now ready to be filled with water. Be careful not to dislodge the plants or stir up the gravel. Let the water stand for about a week to ensure that it has aged and is at room temperature. Then it is ready to support the marine life you choose. In general, plan on 1 inch of aquatic animal per gallon of capacity. For instance, a 10-gallon tank can support two 5-inch salamanders.

You may purchase aquatic life from a reputable dealer (your merit badge counselor can tell you how to find one) or catch some common species from small streams or ponds near your home. You can choose a variety of species for your aquarium, including many kinds of small fish, snails, tadpoles, freshwater shrimp, golden shiners, and water insects like whirligig beetles.

A complete aquarium can now be monitored for changes in life cycles and management issues. When your studies are concluded to your counselor's satisfaction, with your counselor's assistance, determine whether the organisms can be safely returned to their natural environment. Check with your local fish and game agencies, as some species might be harmful and should not be released, while others might be protected and require permits. If you decide to keep your aquarium and organisms for a while longer, don't forget to follow up on this before you release any of your specimens.

Polar bear

Reproduction Rates

Most species of fish and wildlife have the ability to produce far more offspring than the available habitat will support. This is nature's way of assuring that the species will survive and providing energy for other species in the food chain. There are some exceptions; a polar bear generally has two cubs every three years, and a female condor usually produces only a single egg every two years. This might reflect the traditional seasonal availability of food.

High reproductive capability sometimes can work against the best interests of fish and wildlife managers. For example, when many large predatory fish are removed from a lake, smaller fish such as bluegills become overpopulated and

One way that fish are managed is by removing undesirable fish populations using an organic toxin called *rotenone* and releasing desired fish species to replace them.

The white-tailed deer is a species well-known for reproducing at rates far greater than the habitat can support. Unless their numbers are kept under control, generally by natural predators or human hunting, they tend to overpopulate until the food supply is depleted and disease and starvation set in, cycling the population back to below what the habitat can support.

Prescribed fire

deplete the food supply. Without adequate food they fail to grow to a desirable size and are no longer of interest to anglers.

Sometimes a high reproductive capability fails to produce a desirable number of a given species. The American lobster found along the coastal waters of New England is a case in point. An adult female can produce more than 20,000 eggs once every two years, but because the harsh environment, including natural predation, results in only a few lobsters surviving to adulthood, wildlife managers must place strict limits on the harvest of this species.

A **prescribed fire** is a planned and controlled fire set by land managers with the specific purpose of benefiting a specific natural area.

Management Practices

Methods of managing fish and wildlife are highly diverse and are constantly changing. New ideas develop, research produces new fish and wildlife information, land uses change, and growing human populations place ever-increasing pressures on the environment and on Earth's plants and animals. Some of those management practices are discussed here.

As a forest matures, its value for certain wildlife species generally diminishes. The wildlife manager might determine that for wildlife needing early growth forest habitat, trees should be thinned or removed completely *(clear-cut)* to open the way for ground vegetation. This management method also might involve favoring or sometimes even planning a certain selection of trees to provide food and cover for particular species of wildlife.

For the same reason, **prescribed fire** might be required to discourage one kind of vegetation and stimulate the growth of another that is preferred by certain wildlife. Along with removing undesired vegetation, planting a particular kind of plant or mix of certain plants might provide critical habitat needed for

Today, many saltwater recreational fishing trips originating in Texas, Louisiana, and Mississippi head for the offshore drilling rigs in central and western parts of the Gulf of Mexico to harvest the bounty of fish provided by or attracted to the artificial fish habitat.

certain wildlife species. This kind of management often is merely a substitute for natural forces like forest and prairie wildfires that must be controlled in order to protect other resources.

Improving stream habitat for fish might involve installing physical structures like log dams and deflectors, large boulders, and anchored trees. Stream bank vegetation and artificial shelter can be established in inland lakes by immersing brush and discarded Christmas trees.

Offshore oil and gas production platforms have proven to create tremendous artificial fish habitats. In the Gulf of Mexico, there are more than 4,000 such rigs intended primarily for oil and gas production but that also provide a great fishery. The early life stages of numerous algae, coral, barnacles, sponges, and other marine organisms drift in currents until they find a suitable habitat, or die. When they attach to the underwater drilling platform framework, they can **metamorphose** or change into adult forms, grow and propagate, and become a food source for other marine creatures.

For an organism to **metamorphose,** it must have an appropriate habitat in which to change from one body form to another.

Junk automobiles, tires, abandoned barges, and construction rubble are examples of materials that have been used to create artificial reef habitat for fish in both freshwater lakes and coastal areas.

Platforms no longer in use for drilling are increasingly being left in place for use as fishing holes, to substitute or mitigate for environmental damage elsewhere and generally to create habitat for fish and other sea life.

Platform legs also provide shelter from currents and predators, as well as convenient navigational reference points for fish. In essence, they create new habitats and increase the number of animals a given area of ocean can support.

Much the same thing happens on platforms off the California coast. Mussels grow so quickly and abundantly that they must be constantly scraped off so that their added bulk does not cause strong ocean currents to weaken the platform. A Santa Barbara company now harvests thousands of pounds of these mussels every week for sale to four-star restaurants in a number of states. Huge schools of fish also can be found beneath these oil drilling platforms.

Perhaps the best-known management methods are hunting and fishing regulations. Generally the goal is to set regulations so that only harvestable surpluses are removed by hunters and anglers. Breeding populations are then maintained at the optimum numbers the habitat can support.

A **game species** is a species that can be legally hunted in an area.

If too many **game** animals are harvested from a certain area, there would be too few of the species to make maximum use of the habitat (food, water, shelter, space). If too few animals are harvested, the surpluses will run short of habitat and as a result might die because of starvation or disease, and other less desirable species might move in and take over. The situation is not quite as clear-cut with fish, but the idea is basically the same.

Damage Control

Another part of fish and wildlife management consists of damage control—practices to reduce or eliminate conflicts between humans and fish and wildlife.

Almost any animal at times can cause trouble for humans. Some situations are just plain nuisances, like raccoons upsetting trash cans. More serious cases occur when wildlife cause financial losses,

Raccoon

To solve an animal damage problem, wildlife managers often use a combination of safe, selective, effective, and humane control methods. Anyone who needs to resolve a problem between wildlife and people should be sure that the right method is used so that other animals and the environment will not be hurt.

like thousands of blackbirds invading a farmer's cornfield, or coyotes killing sheep, or wild horses and burros overgrazing and destroying the range, thereby making forage unavailable for antelope and other animals. The worst kind of conflict occurs when wildlife threaten the health and safety of humans, like a rabid fox wandering into a schoolyard or a flock of starlings flying a collision course with a jet aircraft.

There are two general methods for reducing these problems. First, the habitat can be made unacceptable for the offending species, forcing it to move to more suitable shelter. Second, the targeted animal or group of animals can be fenced out, repelled, live trapped and released elsewhere, or if necessary, selectively destroyed by the safest and most humane means available. Habitat management usually is the long-term solution, because if an animal is deprived of food, water, shelter, or living space, it will have to move elsewhere or die.

One thing holds true: Conflicts and competition with wildlife will increase as more and more humans displace more and more wildlife habitat.

SUCCESS STORIES

If fish and wildlife management had not been as tremendously successful as it has been, we would be living in quite a different environment today.

By the early 1900s, forests were fast disappearing in the face of massive logging and uncontrolled fires. Rangelands were being overgrazed and were becoming highly eroded. Market hunters were slaughtering wildlife without restriction. The passenger pigeon was almost gone, and relatively few beavers, antelope, whooping cranes, elk, white-tailed deer, wild turkeys, egrets, herons, trumpeter swans, wood ducks, and fur seals remained. It was assumed that all the larger game animals soon would be gone.

Fisheries management is the active knowledge and technology having to do with our fish resources.

Since that time the human population has mushroomed and land-use requirements that exclude fish and wildlife have increased tremendously. However, in spite of all the factors that indicate a continued downward trend in fish and wildlife populations, there are many examples that show the downward trend can be monitored, contained, and in some cases, reversed.

An interesting **fisheries management** story is shared by inland states where striped bass were introduced in many freshwater reservoirs throughout the nation. Like the salmon and steelhead trout, the striped bass is an *anadromous* species—it normally spawns (lays its eggs) in freshwater coastal streams and returns to the ocean and bays to grow and mature. Fisheries managers learned techniques for artificially spawning and rearing striped bass, making it possible to stock this fish in freshwater reservoirs where it reaches trophy sizes of 30 to 60 pounds. Another benefit of stocking striped bass is their ability to consume competing forage and nongame species, resulting in better survival and faster growth rates for the stripers.

Striped bass

Think about the grizzly bear. These hefty creatures will avoid humans whenever possible. However, if surprised, cornered, or separated from offspring, a grizzly bear would not think twice about defending itself. Therefore, to protect both the bear and the public, wildlife managers consider the grizzly's habits and temperament as part of any grizzly bear management plan.

Grizzly bear

Location, Location

Many of us have read stories and seen pictures of the black bear caught in a bear trap at Yellowstone National Park or elsewhere. The trapping and relocation of "nuisance" bears, mountain lions, and other species is as much for the safety and well-being of the animal as it is for the humans it might encounter. The success of this well-accepted program is saving the lives of many animals.

Gray wolf

Through their licensing fees and excise taxes on fishing and hunting equipment, hunters and anglers have paid much of the bill for these restoration efforts.

As a result, very successful tactics have been developed and instituted, including establishing what are called land corridors for grizzly bears. These large passageways allow the bears to travel unhindered over their normally extensive natural range. Oftentimes these corridors may link two separate but vital wilderness areas used by the bears. Such a management plan shows how developing an understanding of the grizzly bear and planning accordingly can help prevent many human-bear incidents.

Many other examples can be cited. Through habitat improvement, improved survey work, and better hunting regulations, many species are more plentiful today than decades ago, even though much of their former habitat has been taken for other uses. White-tailed deer, wild turkeys, and American bison are far more plentiful now, for example, than they were at the turn of the century. Wood ducks, once assumed headed toward extinction, are now plentiful enough so that hunting bag limits and open seasons have been extended.

Modern wildlife management also has been successful in bringing a number of endangered and threatened species from near extinction to comfortable reproducing numbers. The bald eagle is a prime example of success in this area, as is the eastern timber wolf in Yellowstone National Park and Minnesota, and the American alligator in Florida and Louisiana. Throughout the world many species that would be gone by now are still with us, in many cases thriving, because of modern wildlife management techniques.

The Value of Fish and Wildlife

In any discussion of fish and wildlife management and efforts to ensure the existence of creatures in certain numbers throughout the nation, it seems only fair to question why. One answer is that people simply enjoy watching and photographing fish and wildlife, and even enjoy just knowing the creatures exist, even if unseen. Fish and wildlife also help us understand all living things and how all plant and animal life forms exist in relationship to each other. There are many other reasons, but perhaps the most commonly thought of reasons to maintain fish and wildlife are hunting and fishing.

Hunting

In some areas, wildlife managers use hunting as a tool to manage our wildlife resources as well as a source of funds for further wildlife management activities. Hunting also serves as a recreational opportunity for our citizens.

Some of the benefits of hunting are obvious. Hunting can help prevent overpopulation of some species, like deer, that can damage their natural habitat if they become too numerous. Individual deer in overpopulated areas would most likely die of starvation or disease unless harvested by hunters. In addition, the subsequent destruction of habitat from deer overpopulation generally leads to massive losses of many other species because the land can no longer provide sufficient habitat for all those species.

The most significant and obvious benefit of hunting is that it provides millions of sports enthusiasts with an opportunity to enjoy the outdoors.

Wildlife managers use hunting as a tool to help reduce the number of animals in any given area, thereby, for example, minimizing the damage to crops, orchards, and the wildlife habitat in general.

According to the U.S. Fish and Wildlife Service, an estimated 12.5 million people ages 16 and older went hunting in 2006. They spent more than $22.9 billion on equipment, land leases, and other expenses to follow their sport.

Fishing

People were catching fish long before recorded history. Archaeologists discovered that early humans fashioned hooklike devices made of bones, antlers, shells, and stones. One design, called a *gorge*, was nothing more than a short shaft tapered to a point at both ends and was embedded lengthwise in the bait. The line was attached to the middle of the gorge. When the bait was swallowed, the fisherman pulled the attached line, causing the pointed ends of the shaft to lodge in the fish's throat. Later versions consisted of a recurved, single-pointed hook design, which bore a striking resemblance to modern fishhooks.

These early fish catching efforts were intended solely to provide fish for food. Although the earliest time that people first fished for enjoyment as well as food remains shrouded in antiquity, centuries-old prints depicting a man fishing with a pole and line appear often in examples of Chinese art.

The U.S. Fish and Wildlife Service estimates that 34 million Americans went recreational fishing in 2001 and spent more than $35 billion on equipment and outings. The number of fishermen increased at almost twice the rate of the American population since 1955; while the U.S. population is up 71 percent, the percentage of Americans who count fishing among their hobbies is up more than 130 percent.

The quantity and diversity of fish habitat is undoubtedly the main reason for the highly successful commercial fishing industry and the popularity of recreational fishing in the United States, which has more than 90,000 miles of tidal shoreline and more than 300 species of commercially harvested fish. Freshwater fishing is available in lakes, ponds, rivers, and streams scattered across the country from coast to coast and border to border.

More than half the U.S. population now resides in a coastal area. This puts tremendous stress on our fragile coastal ecosystem. Professional fish and wildlife managers and other concerned citizens are taking responsibility for maintaining this excellent fishery resource. They have kept a watchful eye on our varied fishery habitat and fish populations in general. For one reason, as we become more and more industrialized, we are increasingly threatened with pollution that can ruin

It is easy to see that the management of all our fishery resources will be a highly challenging and rewarding career activity in the years ahead.

our waters. Also, as populations grow and fishing equipment becomes more and more sophisticated, we put a greater stress on our fish populations.

Observing

While many wildlife enthusiasts are avid hunters and anglers, many others pursue their wildlife interests by way of other hobbies. Some compile life lists as bird-watchers. Others engage in fish and wildlife photography and art, both as artists and collectors. Still others develop backyard habitats such as nesting boxes, ponds, and plantings of vegetation for food and shelter.

Many avid anglers and hunters develop additional, related fish and wildlife interests.

Brown pelican

We know now that very small amounts of some pesticides eaten by brown pelicans, bald eagles, peregrine falcons, and many other species may kill them or make them unable to produce young. These three species nearly became extinct some years back through wide use of a chemical known as DDT. This pesticide found its way into their diets and caused their eggs to develop only thin, fragile shells. Their thin-shelled eggs tended to break in the nest before the young were hatched, causing a rapid and drastic decline in population of these species. Loss of wildlife habitat by draining and filling wetlands (marshes, sloughs, and swamps), building dams on rivers and streams, clearing land, or building cities and airports can have an enormous impact on animals that are not able to adjust to a new or changed environment.

Endangered Species

Abrupt changes give sensitive wildlife species no time to adapt and no place to retreat.

Hunting, fishing, and other values of fish and wildlife are obvious uses that provide food, hobbies, and simple enjoyment. The subject of **endangered** species represents a very real value, though perhaps more subtle and complex. The principal reason animals are becoming endangered at an ever-increasing rate is that people are causing major changes in the natural environment. Because many animals have very specific habitat requirements, what appears to be a minor change to humans might be devastating to the animal.

Humpback whale

Endangered means that only a few individuals of a species remain alive. They are in danger of becoming extinct. **Extinct** means that not one individual of a species is still alive. The word **threatened** is used to describe a species that is almost endangered.

During the past few hundred years when the human population has skyrocketed, the extinction process has accelerated drastically. Some animals became endangered species because they competed with people. Wolves and grizzly bears are examples of animals that were deliberately killed because they fed on domestic livestock.

Some of the whales, sea turtles, alligators, crocodiles, spotted cats, and other species have been reduced to the endangered status because of their considerable commercial

Desert bighorn sheep

Birds and animals that are native to islands are especially vulnerable to introduced predators. For example, just a few years ago the brown tree snake gained access to the Island of Guam in the North Pacific. In just a short time these large tree-climbing snakes virtually wiped out the flourishing bird populations.

About 40 percent of Hawaii's native birds are now extinct; another 40 percent, like the nene goose (pictured here), are endangered.

An **exotic species** is any plant or animal that is not naturally occurring in an area. An **invasive species** is an exotic that spreads rapidly and competes with native species.

value. Others, like the badlands bighorn sheep, Merriams elk, and eastern elk were exterminated by meat and trophy hunters prior to 1910. Many of these extinct animals were destroyed before most people thought seriously about conservation.

The introduction of foreign (or **exotic**) animals has resulted in the loss of a number of our native species. Introduced birds and animals such as European starlings and rats, introduced diseases, and overgrazing and foraging by sheep and cattle have drastically affected native animals and their habitats.

The same causes that contribute to the endangered status of mammals and birds also generally apply to fish. Harmful environmental change brought about by human activity is thought to be the most important cause. In fact, fish are even more vulnerable than mammals or birds, as most fish are captives of their stream or lake habitats. They are unable to move at will to the next mountain or valley if disturbed by human activity. On the brighter side, some success has been achieved in recent years for improving chances for survival of several endangered species.

A number of fish species once included on the endangered list have been reclassified as threatened, a less critical category, though still indicating the need for continued protection. A few examples of such "downlisted" species include Alabama

Why should people try to save endangered species, sometimes at a considerable cost? Perhaps the answer is that extinction is *final*. If people are responsible for endangering an animal, they have an obligation to future generations of humans to try to save that animal. Furthermore, it is in our interest to preserve all species, because a variety of living things provides a greater diversity of social, recreational, scientific, and economic benefits for everyone.

cavefish, snail darter, and Apache trout. Some of these species were at least partially restored as a result of successful transplants to new and undisturbed habitats where they have a better chance to survive. Others have benefited from habitat improvement and the adoption of more protective regulations. Endangered fishes reared at fish hatcheries will be useful in future restoration programs.

Environmental Barometers

A somewhat subtle fish and wildlife value is that the creatures serve humans as environmental barometers. A barometer is an instrument used to help forecast weather.

Years ago, coal miners carried caged canaries with them into deep underground mines. Someone kept a constant sharp eye on the bird, because its behavior reflected the condition of the air. Canaries are much more sensitive to impure air than humans. If the canary died, the miners headed for the surface because deadly methane gas was probably present.

In much more subtle ways, fish and wildlife can serve to measure the quality of the environment. Clear, cool streams that ought to support trout, but do not, suggest something may be drastically wrong with the quality of the water. Similarly, the populations of frogs and other amphibians have experienced a significant drop in numbers globally. This trend has signaled an environmental concern among scientists.

Ideally, we should strive to assure that most species remain in abundance. If this were the case, the quality of the environment for humans would be healthy, too.

The presence or absence of fish and wildlife can reflect the way people live and how well or how poorly they are treating the environment.

A fish die-off is often the first sign of pollution in a water supply.

Help Curb Invasive Species

Over eons of time, populations of plant and animal species develop complex relationships in balance with nature. This delicate balance can easily be destroyed when an invasive species enters the picture.

When nonnative, exotic plants and animals are introduced into an ecosystem, they often have no natural predators or controls to keep them in check with the established habitat. Such an environment allows them to aggressively spread out and compete with native species for food, water, shelter, and space, and to expose these native species to new diseases and other hazards. This is why invasive species are a major threat to nature—and also to recreational areas such as lakes and parks that we all enjoy.

You can help curb the effects of invasive species. Remember that people and human activity are the major transporters of invasive species.

- After a hike, shake out your socks and remove any weeds and seeds from your shoes before heading home.

- When you are through boating, inspect your equipment and boat before leaving the site. You don't want to transport any plants, water, mud, leftover bait, or fish and other living things to another area.

- If you have caught any fish, release it back only to the area where it was caught. Never transport your catch and release it somewhere else. In addition, never release anything from your home aquarium to a lake, pond, or other body of water.

- If you are riding a bike, motorcycle, horse, or any other transportation across long distances, be sure you don't pick up any "hitchhikers" along the way, such as seeds, plant parts, and bugs.

Here are only a few examples of invasive species. You might recognize them.

Phragmites are a wild, cane-like plant that dominates thousands of acres of coastal and interior wetlands. It spreads readily, forming vast and dense reed beds that choke out native plant species. The stalks and plumes of phragmites can grow to around 14 feet high, making it even more difficult to control and eliminate.

The invasive **island apple snail** came from the aquarium and aquaculture trades via South America. This agricultural pest grows to about the size of a baseball, devours any type of aquatic plant, has few natural enemies, and multiplies quickly. In fact, one female island apple snail can lay up to 1,000 eggs every 10 to 14 days.

The eerie looking **snakehead fish** escaped from the aquarium pet trade and fish markets into local waterways, where it has spread rapidly, eating up native fish and their eggs. During droughts, snakeheads can actually wriggle over land on their fins and body to reach other waterways. Outside their native habitat, they have no known enemies.

Phragmites

Island apple snail

Snakehead fish

Who's Responsible for Fish and Wildlife?

In a very real sense the responsibility for fish and wildlife must be shared by everybody, but officially this responsibility belongs to public agencies.

The U.S. Fish and Wildlife Service within the Department of the Interior has primary responsibility for the management of migratory birds (ducks, geese, robins, and woodpeckers, for example); for endangered and threatened species (whooping cranes, California condors, grizzly bears); and for some marine mammals (polar bears, walruses, and sea otters). A major part of the service's responsibility for these groups of wildlife takes place on habitat within the National Wildlife Refuge System. More than 540 refuges, totaling more than 95 million acres, represent the largest system of lands and waters in the world devoted to the management of wildlife and wildlife habitat.

The Department of Commerce, through its National Marine Fisheries Service, is responsible for providing the scientific and technical information needed to conserve, manage, and develop living marine resources. The information and analyses they provide are the basis for management and development decisions that support the growth and stability of the U.S. recreational and commercial marine fishing industries and protection of endangered aquatic species.

Each of the 50 state governments has a conservation department or game and fish division with the responsibility of managing the state's resident fish and wildlife species. In all, some 50 million acres of habitat are managed by the states for fish and wildlife, both game and nongame species.

A similar arrangement between the states and federal government exists for fish. The federal government has a responsibility for managing fisheries in international water and in waters contained on federal lands. The states manage the fisheries in inland waters contained within the states.

Other federal land management agencies, such as the USDA Forest Service, the National Park Service, and the Bureau of Land Management, administer millions of acres of public lands. They also have responsibilities for wildlife by virtue of their management of these lands.

FISH AND WILDLIFE MANAGEMENT 39

Continue Your Interest

As you continue to develop your interest in fish and wildlife, it might become a very enriching part of your life. You will come to realize that our nation is blessed with an amazing amount of highly diversified fish and wildlife habitat, much of it publicly owned so that it can be enjoyed by all Americans. Those who become heavily involved in fish and wildlife conservation tend to develop a deep pride in our public lands. They often serve as volunteers for local habitat improvement projects, in litter clean-up efforts, reporting vandalism, supporting conservation organizations, and preventing various forms of misuse and abuse.

As a parting thought: Hundreds of years from now, future generations also will cherish fish and wildlife resources just as many of us do today. If you elect to devote some of your time and energy helping to conserve and improve fish and wildlife habitats, you will undoubtedly gain a deep sense of satisfaction in assuring these enjoyable benefits for future generations.

Besides government programs, many other organizations contribute significantly to our nation's fish and wildlife management efforts (see the resources section at the end of this pamphlet). In fact, many private foundations and nonprofit conservation organizations protect and manage lands that provide valuable habitat for all kinds of wildlife. These lands may serve as nesting sites and feeding zones for wetland waterfowl and migratory birds, or as corridors or buffer zones between fish or wildlife habitats and human developments, or they may house rehabilitation programs for injured and disaster-affected animals (such as from oil spills), to name a few. Many private foundations also conduct research on specific fish and wildlife species, sharing valuable input with wildlife managers all over the world.

For most Scouts who earn the Fish and Wildlife Management merit badge, the knowledge gained will be the beginning of a wonderful lifetime hobby rather than a career. Wherever you end up living, there will be opportunities for you to continue to learn about fish and wildlife and to be active in conservation pursuits. National, state, and local organizations offer memberships and activities in this field, and if you are typical, others who share your interests will become lifelong friends.

Observe, Listen, and Learn

The best way to learn about fish and wildlife is to get outdoors and experience it. One can quickly find out the types of materials a squirrel prefers for its nest, for example. Over time, observers can notice such things as migratory patterns and the effect of human influence on a habitat. Always remember, though, that this Earth is the only one we have—do your best to leave it the way you found it by following the principles of Leave No Trace.

Safety

Nearly all animals will avoid people if they can. However, some wildlife can be especially dangerous if the animal is protecting its young. Always be careful when observing wild animals. Never go out alone if there is the possibility of encountering bears or mountain lions.

Principles of Leave No Trace

Do your part to keep nature natural by following these principles.

1. Plan ahead and prepare. Proper planning and preparation increases safety, reduces the impact of your visit on the environment, and helps make your outdoor experience more enjoyable.

2. Travel and camp on durable surfaces. Natural environments are easily damaged by foot traffic. Use existing trails or travel on durable surfaces such as rock, gravel, sand, compacted soil, dry grasses, or snow. Large groups should spread out to avoid creating new trails. Keep campsites small.

3. Dispose of waste properly (pack it in, pack it out). Any material people leave behind pollutes the environment and might create a health hazard for wildlife or other visitors. Pack out any trash and leftover food. Dispose of human waste by digging catholes 6 to 8 inches deep and 200 feet away from water, trails, and campsites.

4. Leave what you find. Observe the interesting things you find, but do not disturb them. Use established campsites and do not alter them in any way. Restore campsites to pristine condition before you leave.

5. Minimize campfire impacts. Use a lightweight stove when cooking in the backcountry. If you need to build a fire, keep it small and use only dead or downed wood. Never cut down limbs or trees for firewood.

6. Respect wildlife. Stay far enough away from animals that your presence does not disturb their natural activity. Store food, food scraps, and trash securely to prevent animals from eating food that is not part of their natural diet. Never feed animals.

7. Be considerate of other visitors. Let everyone enjoy nature. Travel and camp quietly and away from other people. Blend in by wearing subdued colors. Leave pets and portable audio devices at home.

Types of Wildlife

Take some time to learn a little about the types of wildlife and fish that can be found in the wild, then go out and watch them. This will help you determine their needs and could possibly give you an idea for a project that will improve their habitat.

Mammals

Mammals are the only animals on Earth that nurse their young. They are warm-blooded, which helps them adapt to all kinds of climates. They also are intelligent. If you could give an IQ test to every species of animal, mammals would score higher than all other animals.

You are likely to spot a variety of mammals in any wildlife community. Being familiar with some animals' habits will give you a greater chance of observing them in the wild. A large percentage of mammals are *nocturnal*—that is, they stay in their dens or burrows during the day, venturing out for food at night. Hoofed animals, like the deer and sheep, usually are found in more open wild areas, where they can feed on grasses and leaves. Wooded areas are home to many types of mammals, including members of the rodent family that live among

State fish and wildlife agencies can provide information on exotic animals, game species, furbearers, and migratory game birds that includes a list of currently endangered animals that live in your area.

The Arctic hare's natural camouflage helps it blend into its environment and evade predators.

Beaver-eaten tree

Most mammals are too shy to come out of their natural camouflage and put themselves on display, so spotting them is not easy. If you start looking for tracks or other signs, though, you will find that mammals are much more common than you think. Look for the following signs:

- Tracks in the mud or sand along waterways
- Signs of feeding around fruit-bearing shrubs or trees
- Rough bark around the hole in a hollow tree
- Droppings on animal runways in woods or fields
- Animal homes—holes in the ground, muskrat houses, or beaver dams

the leaf litter on the forest floor or in tunnels under lawns and fields. You might sight a water mammal if you live near an ocean; whales, seals, sea lions, sea otters, walruses, porpoises, and dolphins all breathe air and must surface frequently for a fresh supply.

Predatory mammals, including flesh-eaters like bears, raccoons, skunks, opossums, foxes, wolves, and bobcats, are found in every kind of wildlife community. Some of them eat plants, but all prefer to eat other animals and have canine teeth for tearing flesh.

Birds

The best way to learn to identify birds is to venture outside and look and listen for them. Borrow a pair of binoculars to make watching more fun and identifying the birds easier. Then, learn something about bird families and where they usually are found so that you will be able to identify any bird you see.

American kestrel

If you are near a lake or a river, you might very well see ducks, geese, wading birds like herons or egrets, or shore birds like sandpipers or killdeer. If you are near the ocean, you might see gulls or terns. An area with lots of trees could be home to woodpeckers, flycatchers, jays, warblers, and orioles. Prairies and fields are good habitat for swallows, thrashers, thrushes, and meadowlarks. In almost all wildlife communities, bird watchers can find finches and sparrows.

As you watch birds, find out as much as you can about them. To help you determine a bird's species and to recognize it the next time you see it, take note of its call, size, shape, and habitat, as well as its song, what it eats, how it flies, the trees or other plants it favors, where it nests, whether it walks or hops, and specific markings such as an eye stripe, wingbars, and coloration.

American robin

Reptiles and Amphibians

Once you learn the differences between reptiles and amphibians, you can easily tell them apart. Reptiles include snakes, lizards, turtles, alligators, and crocodiles, while salamanders, frogs, toads, and newts are amphibians. Reptiles hatch or are born on land and look just like their parents, but most amphibians spend their early life in the water and go through extreme changes on their way to adulthood. Amphibians can live on land or in water, while most reptiles are more terrestrial.

Desert tortoise

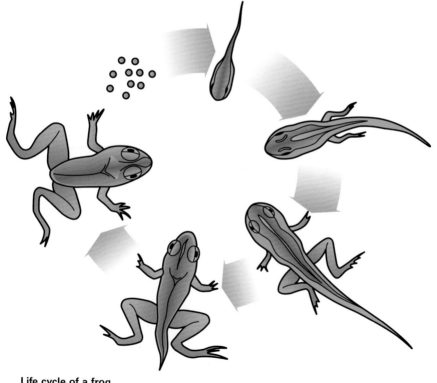

Life cycle of a frog

The best time to look for reptiles and amphibians is in the spring, as they emerge from hibernation seeking food, the warmth of the sun, and their mates. Fall usually is the next best season to see reptiles, as they seek sunshine for warmth again; many gather near dens or burrows. Summer searching is unpredictable. You might find turtles, water snakes, and many varieties of frogs during hot weather, but most shun the heat and the sun. Others prowl only at night; sometimes it is worthwhile to look for them with a flashlight after dark. In areas with harsh winters, these animals hibernate during the cold weather and cannot be found.

When looking for reptiles and amphibians, leave no stone unturned. Tip up and then make sure to replace all objects beneath which something might hide, including boards, flat or loose rocks, cracks in cliffs and ledges, rock slabs, and boulders. Peeling the bark away from rotten logs or tearing logs or stumps apart also can help; the sudden light temporarily dazzles the uncovered animal to give you a chance to identify it.

Broad-banded copperhead

While most reptiles are harmless and all are beneficial, a few (like the broad-banded copperhead shown here) can be dangerous. There are four groups of poisonous snakes, one poisonous lizard, and a few large turtles that can inflict painful bites. There are poisonous snakes in nearly every state in the country.

Frogs and toads have distinctive calls. Some, like the spring peeper, have a high, piping noise. Others, like the leopard, wood, and pickerel frogs, make a noise that sounds like a snore or a grunt; the call of the green frog resembles a loose mandolin string; and the bullfrog's low "jug-o-rum" is well-known to almost everyone.

Catch and release is an important conservation measure practiced by fishermen. In some areas, catch and release is the law. See the *Fishing* or *Fly-Fishing* merit badge pamphlets for more information on the sport.

Fish

Fish can be found just about anywhere there is water. Whether as small as a backyard pond or as large as an ocean, bodies of water are home to fish of all shapes and sizes. Some freshwater fish you might catch include bass, panfish, catfish, and trout. If you live near a coastal area, try fishing for saltwater fish such as yellowtail, drum, pompano, redfish, salmon, snapper, and spotted sea trout.

A few tips could make finding a place to catch fish in freshwater or saltwater easy. Fish like edges, so look for them where the bank meets the water, where a sandbar drops off, and where two currents meet. Fish like to hide, too. Look around weed beds; underneath overhanging trees, brush, and docks; and where rocks jut out from shore. Fish like rapids and currents. Rushing water carries food and lots of oxygen, both of which fish enjoy. Look for fish in pools under waterfalls.

You Are What You Eat

Optional requirement 7c asks you to examine the stomach contents of three fish. As an angler, doing so will tell you what that species feeds on in the wild—insects, worms, smaller fish, vegetation, and so on. It will give you a good idea of the best bait or lure to use. Resource managers use this same information to help ensure that the species has access to the most appropriate food sources.

Examining a fish's entrails can be done easily when cleaning a fish you intend to eat. If you are not able to visit a cleaning station or to find a similar alternative, you may need to gut a fish yourself. (For tips on safe knife use, review your *Boy Scout Handbook*.) After skinning or scaling the fish, follow these steps.

Step 1—Starting at the anal opening near the tail, cut through the skin from the belly to the gills. Be careful not to cut too deeply and destroy the organs.

Step 2—Open the belly and use your fingers to carefully remove the gills from the fish. Scrape out the kidney line (it's reddish brown) along the backbone. Detach the entrails from the fish by cutting them away from the fish's body; be careful not to burst the stomach.

Remember to responsibly dispose of all remains. Follow Leave No Trace principles, and treat this waste as you would human waste by either packing it out or burying it in a cathole that is 6 to 8 inches deep and at least 200 feet from the water source, trails, or campsites.

SCALES

SCALE

Once you land a fish, you can learn a lot about it by sampling a single scale, including its age. Like trees, a fish's scales show rings that give away its age. As the fish grows, its scales grow with it, leaving behind circular ridges—widely placed in warm months and closely placed in cooler months. As the seasons pass, each band of wide and close ridges marks one year of a fish's life.

To take a scale sample from a fish, choose a mature scale from behind the dorsal fin toward the top of the fish. Slip needle-nose pliers under a scale and gently tug toward the fish's tail. Any scale that is removed can be regenerated by the fish, so the live fish may be released once your sample is taken. Growth seasons can be counted by rings on the scale, much like the growth rings on a tree.

Conducting a Creel Census

The results of a creel census are helpful in estimating the number of fish the average angler catches in an hour at one body of water. A simple survey will help compile the data. As anglers return to the dock after a day of fishing, poll them about their catch. How many hours were they out, and how many fish did they catch? The more anglers you poll, the more accurate your results will be.

Observing Wildlife

A simple way to help make your backyard more inviting to wildlife observation is to replace exotic plants with those that are native to the region. Some ways to attract and pamper local wildlife include adding birdbaths filled with clean, fresh water, using natural insecticides rather than chemicals, building brush piles, and planting native trees. When you go into the wild to observe wildlife, though, follow these tips.

Blend Into the Landscape

Find a comfortable spot to sit or lie prone. Stay absolutely still and be patient. Some animals will lose their fear of you after a time and venture out of hiding. If you want to make your presence even less obvious, build a blind one day and go into it a day or two later when the animals have gotten used to it. Take binoculars if you have them.

Go Out at Night

With your parent or another Scout, visit a natural habitat at night. Take a flashlight. Shine the light at intervals on the trail ahead, into treetops, and into dense brush. Skunks, foxes, deer, flying squirrels, raccoons, and opossums might be looking at you.

Take to the Water

Look along a stream bank or lakeshore for tracks in the mud and sand. That night, go out in a boat with a flashlight and row to a point offshore from where you saw the tracks. Sit quietly, and at the slightest sound, aim your light toward it. Or anchor near a beaver dam or muskrat house and shine your light whenever you hear a sound.

Stake Out a Burrow

If you spot a hole in the ground while on a hike, poke some pencil-sized sticks lightly into the ground around it. If the hole is a mammal's burrow, you will find the sticks knocked down when you come back to look at it later. So sit down in a comfortable spot nearby and wait. If you are patient, you might be rewarded by a look at a woodchuck, badger, ground squirrel, pocket gopher, or chipmunk.

Look Along the Edges

As you observe wildlife communities, you will discover that the best places to find animals are where two communities meet. This edge attracts more wildlife than either of the communities. Here, you will find a greater variety of plants, which supply more food and more cover for more animals.

For example, rabbits find food in fields where clover grows, but they need tangle or brush for cover from their enemies. Where a field meets a shrubby wood, rabbits have food and cover close together and therefore can live successfully.

However, even though a greater variety of wildlife can be found along the edge, some animals avoid the edges and require large stretches of a certain type of terrain, such as an unbroken forest.

Where a prairie meets a woodland, where a hay field meets a cornfield, where a marsh blends into woods, or wherever two communities come together, you will find a larger variety of animals.

Anything that you can use to conceal yourself can be used as a blind. A tent, a hollow tree, or a cave might serve well. Set up your blind downwind from the spot where you expect the animals to come. Camouflage the blind with branches, grasses, and reeds to make it look as much a part of the landscape as possible.

Nest Boxes

The types of homes for different species are, of course, different. Installing a nest box that is specially suited for a particular animal might give you the best opportunity to observe the animals without disturbing them. Nest boxes need to be maintained by cleaning them out once a year.

Squirrels and raccoons normally make their homes from large cavities in trees or hollow logs. You can make them a good home by fitting a wooden nail keg with a "roof" and an entrance hole. Place the hole on the side for easy entrance, and cut the entrance hole a little larger for bigger mammals like the raccoon. A raccoon box should be placed in a wooded area not too far from water, while a squirrel box belongs in an oak or nut tree woodland.

Squirrel nest box

Many birds, like the Eastern bluebird, make their homes in the hollow of a tree, while other birds are content to build their nests anywhere among its branches. Robins, phoebes, and barn swallows will nest on square wooden platforms mounted beneath the eaves of barns, sheds, or buildings, out of the wind and rain.

A good way to attract birds to your backyard is to provide water. A simple, old-fashioned birdbath works well. Keep it clean by scrubbing it every day or two with hot water and adding fresh water with a hose. Otherwise, the standing water will begin to attract mosquitoes. You need only the bowl from a birdbath or a shallow plastic dish like those made to go under potted plants. Place the bowl directly on the ground near escape cover such as trees or bushes.

Raccoon nest box

Put a flat rock as big as your hand in the middle of the bowl so that only an inch or so of water covers it. Some birds do not like to wade into deep water to bathe and can stand on the rock.

Eastern Bluebird Nest Box

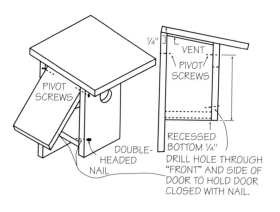

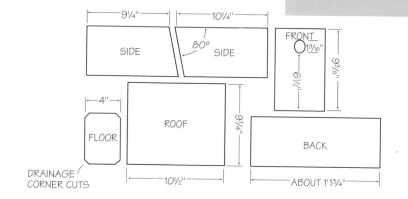

Eastern Bluebird Nest Box Materials List

- ☐ Standard 1" X 6", 4 feet long
- ☐ Standard board 1" X 10", 10½" long
- ☐ 1¾" galvanized nails, approximately 20
- ☐ Two 1¾" galvanized screws for pivot point
- ☐ One double-headed nail for holding door closed

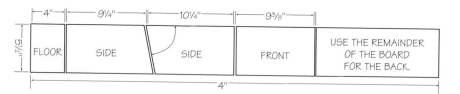

The nest box plans have been provided by the North American Bluebird Society. For more information about bluebirds and their conservation, visit the NABS Web site: *http://www.nabluebirdsociety.org/.*

Careers in Fish and Wildlife Management

If you are already serious about a career in fish and wildlife management, earning this merit badge is the perfect introduction to the subject. Becoming a professional in the fish and wildlife management field offers great challenges and personal satisfaction. To pursue such a career, you should have a strong interest in natural resources and the related sciences.

Wildlife biologist

Zoologist

Fish hatchery
superintendent

Hydrographer

Wildlife manage-
ment consultant

Conservation officer

Oceanographer

Fish and
game warden

Outdoor recreation
planner

Watershed manager

Forest or
park ranger

Environmental
analyst

Soil conservationist

Fisheries officer

Fish and wildlife
technician

Wildlife education
officer

Tree farm manager

Environmental
interpreter

Conservation
educator

Mammalogist

Conservation
law enforcement
officer

However, many people involved in fish and wildlife management are not professional biologists. Many of them are professionals in other fields who combine their abilities with a basic knowledge of and interest in fish and wildlife management. For example, fish and wildlife agencies include on their staffs lawyers, office administrators, writers, engineers, foresters, and other experts. It is a challenging career field, but opportunities are always available for those who have the drive and are willing to work hard.

Preparing for such a career begins when you are still in school. Taking courses in geography, math, history, biology, and physical and social sciences will help you build a strong base. Depending on the field you choose, you most likely will need to develop technical writing skills—especially if your work involves research.

Those who are serious about a career in the field of fish and wildlife management know that the competition for positions is stiff. This makes getting good grades in school and a solid college education essential. Begin by pursuing a broad-based education that strengthens your understanding of natural resources as well as the social, economic, and political forces that affect how decisions are made. Introductory courses in subjects such as wildlife, zoology, math, statistics, computer science, English composition, and botany all are practical. Depending on your major, as you become more focused on a specific area, courses in embryology, taxonomy, genetics, and vertebrate and invertebrate zoology will enhance your understanding of conservation-related fields.

Most conservationists also are public speakers. They might be called to address student groups, civic and service clubs, and other organizations and gatherings. So, get involved with the debate team at school and take courses in public speaking and communication to add value to your education.

Starting early with volunteer work also is a great way to gain valuable experience while making friends and contacts in the profession. Contact your local fish and wildlife service to inquire about volunteer opportunities.

Keep in mind that career opportunities abound in fish and wildlife management not only in the government (city, county, state, federal) and nonprofit sectors but increasingly in the private sector, too. More and more private utility, mining, lumber, and paper companies are employing specialists in the field. Chances are good that you will find a lifelong career that is personally rewarding and enjoyable. For more specific information about education and training requirements and career opportunities, check out the many resources in the back of this pamphlet.

Park naturalist

Teacher

Fisheries biologist

Marine resources technician

College or university professor

Recreation specialist

Wildlife officer

Ornithologist

Parks planning technician

Public information specialist

Resource manager

Planning officer

Lumberyard manager

Equipment operator

Refuge manager

Forester

Park superintendent

Environmental educator

Zookeeper/curator

Veterinarian

Fish and Wildlife Resources

Scouting Literature

Boy Scout Journal; Boy Scout Handbook; Fieldbook; Animal Science, Bird Study, Camping, Environmental Science, Fishing, Fly-Fishing, Forestry, Insect Study, Mammal Study, Nature, Oceanography, Pets, Reptile and Amphibian Study, Soil and Water Conservation, and Veterinary Medicine merit badge pamphlets

Visit the Boy Scouts of America's official retail Web site at http://www.scoutstuff.org for a complete listing of all merit badge pamphlets and other helpful Scouting materials and supplies.

Books

Arnosky, Jim. Field Trips: Bug Hunting, Animal Tracking, Bird-Watching, Shore Walking. HarperCollins Publishers, 2002.

Behler, John. Reptiles (The National Audubon Society First Field Guide). Scholastic Trade, 1999.

Cassie, Brian. Amphibians (The National Audubon Society First Field Guide). Scholastic Trade, 1999.

Chinery, Michael, ed. The Kingfisher Illustrated Encyclopedia of Animals: From Aardvark to Zorille—and 2,000 Other Animals. Kingfisher Books, 1992.

Forsyth, Adrian. Mammals of North America: Temperate and Arctic Regions. Firefly Books LTD, 1999.

Griggs, Jack, ed. All the Birds of North America: American Bird Conservancy's Field Guide. HarperCollins, 1997.

Leopold, Aldo. A Sand County Almanac, reissue ed. Ballantine Books, 1990.

Maynard, Thane. Working With Wildlife: A Guide to Careers in the Animal World. Orchard Books, 2000.

Sayre, April Pulley. Put On Some Antlers and Walk Like a Moose: How Scientists Find, Follow, and Study Wild Animals. Millbrook Press, 1997.

Vergoth, Karin, and Christopher Lampton. Endangered Species. Scholastic Library Publishing, 2000.

Wernert, Susan J., ed. Reader's Digest North American Wildlife. Reader's Digest Adult, 1998.

Organizations and Web Sites

American Birding Association
4945 N. 30th St., Suite 200
Colorado Springs, CO 80919
Toll-free telephone: 800-850-2473
Web site:
http://www.americanbirding.org

American Fisheries Society
5410 Grosvenor Lane
Bethesda, MD 20814
Telephone: 301-897-8616
Web site: *http://www.fisheries.org*

Association of Fish and Wildlife Agencies
444 North Capitol St. NW, Suite 725
Washington, DC 20001
Telephone: 202-624-7890
Web site: *http://www.fishwildlife.org*

Leave No Trace Center for Outdoor Ethics
P.O. Box 997
Boulder, CO 80306
Toll-free telephone: 800-332-4100
Web site: *http://www.lnt.org*

National Audubon Society
700 Broadway
New York, NY 10003
Telephone: 212-979-3000
Web site: *http://www.audubon.org*

National Fish and Wildlife Foundation
1120 Connecticut Ave. NW, Suite 900
Washington, DC 20036
Telephone: 202-857-0166
Web site: *http://www.nfwf.org*

National Marine Fisheries Service
Web site: *http://www.nmfs.noaa.gov*

National Wildlife Federation
11100 Wildlife Center Drive
Reston, VA 20190
Toll-free telephone: 800-822-9919
Web site: *http://www.nwf.org*

National Zoological Park
3001 Connecticut Ave. NW
Washington, DC 20008
Telephone: 202-633-4800
Web site: *http://nationalzoo.si.edu*

The Nature Conservancy
4245 North Fairfax Drive, Suite 100
Arlington, VA 22203-1606
Toll-free telephone: 800-628-6860
Web site: *http://www.nature.org*

U.S. Fish and Wildlife Service
Toll-free telephone: 800-344-9453
Web site: *http://www.fws.gov*

Wildlife Conservation Society
2300 Southern Blvd.
Bronx, NY 10460
Telephone: 718-220-5100
Web site: *http://wcs.org*

Acknowledgements

This edition of the *Fish and Wildlife Management* merit badge pamphlet was prepared by the Boy Scouts of America's national Conservation task force. Special thanks to task force member Gary M. Stolz, Ph.D., who is with the U.S. Fish and Wildlife Service. Dr. Stolz's input, expertise, and accommodating support have been a tremendous help.

The BSA is especially grateful to task force members Daniel A. Poole, president, Wildlife Management Institute; and Harvey K. Nelson, U.S. Fish and Wildlife Service, North American Waterfowl Plan; for their efforts in preparing this new edition. We appreciate the Quicklist Consulting Committee of the Association for Library Service to Children, a division of the American Library Association, for its assistance with updating the resources section of this merit badge pamphlet.

Photo and Illustration Credits

Florida Department of Environmental Protection/Dana Denson, courtesy—page 37 *(island apple snail)*

©Jupiterimages.com—pages 21 and 42

©Photos.com—cover *(all except merit badge and bird box);* pages 14 *(bottom),* 21, 24, 36, and 42

U.S. Department of Agriculture/Bob Nichols, courtesy—page 22

U.S. Fish and Wildlife Service, courtesy—pages 10, 23, 27, and 44

U.S. Fish and Wildlife Service/Erwin and Peggy Bauer, courtesy—page 4 *(top)*

U.S. Fish and Wildlife Service/Tracy Brooks, courtesy—page 4 *(center)*

U.S. Fish and Wildlife Service/Bill Buchanan, courtesy—page 37 *(phragmites)*

U.S. Fish and Wildlife Service/George Gentry, courtesy—page 56

U.S. Fish and Wildlife Service/Bill Gill, courtesy—page 8

U.S. Fish and Wildlife Service/John and Karen Hollingsworth, courtesy—pages 32 and 34

U.S. Fish and Wildlife Service/Robin Hunter, courtesy—page 33 *(top)*

U.S. Fish and Wildlife Service/Beth Jackson, courtesy—page 47 *(top)*

U.S. Fish and Wildlife Service/Lee Karney, courtesy—page 46 *(bottom)*

U.S. Fish and Wildlife Service/K. A. King, courtesy—page 11 *(top)*

U.S. Fish and Wildlife Service/Dave Menke, courtesy—pages 12–13 *(both),* and 46 *(top)*

U.S. Fish and Wildlife Service/LuRay Parker, courtesy—page 57

U.S. Fish and Wildlife Service/Ray Rauch, courtesy—page 48

U.S. Fish and Wildlife Service/Duane Raver, courtesy—page 26 *(top)*

U.S. Fish and Wildlife Service; photo by Robert S. Simmons, courtesy—page 4 *(bottom)*

U.S. Fish and Wildlife Service; photo by Tom Stehn, courtesy—page 11 *(bottom)*

FISH AND WILDLIFE RESOURCES

U.S. Fish and Wildlife Service; photo
by Gary M. Stolz, courtesy—
page 33 *(bottom)*

U.S. Fish and Wildlife Service/Terry
Tollefsbol, courtesy—
page 26 *(bottom)*

U.S. Geological Survey, courtesy—
page 37 *(snakehead fish)*

All other photos and illustrations not
mentioned above are the property of
or are protected by the Boy Scouts
of America.

Gene Daniels—page 59

Daniel Giles—cover *(bird box)*

Vince Heptig—page 9

John McDearmon—pages 17–18
(both), 47 *(illustration)*, 49, 51
(both), and 54–55 *(illustrations)*

Brian Payne—pages 6, 30, and 38

Randy Piland—page 20

Mickey Welsh—pages 31 and 64 *(top)*